John Greenleaf Whittier

The Bay of Seven Islands

And Other Poems

John Greenleaf Whittier

The Bay of Seven Islands
And Other Poems

ISBN/EAN: 9783744704823

Printed in Europe, USA, Canada, Australia, Japan

Cover: Foto ©Thomas Meinert / pixelio.de

More available books at **www.hansebooks.com**

Yours truly

John G. Whittier

THE

BAY OF SEVEN ISLANDS,

AND OTHER POEMS.

BY

JOHN GREENLEAF WHITTIER.

BOSTON:
HOUGHTON, MIFFLIN AND COMPANY.
New York: 11 East Seventeenth Street
The Riverside Press, Cambridge.
1883.

CONTENTS.

CONTENTS.

To H. P. S.

FROM the green Amesbury hill which bears
    the name
Of that half mythic ancestor of mine
Who trod its slopes two hundred years ago,
Down the long valley of the Merrimac
Midway between me and the river's mouth,
I see thy home, set like an eagle's nest
Among Deer Island's immemorial pines,
Crowning the crag on which the sunset breaks
Its last red arrow. Many a tale and song,
Which thou hast told or sung, I call to mind,
Softening with silvery mist the woods and hills,
The out-thrust headlands and in-reaching bays
Of our northeastern coast-line, trending where
The Gulf, midsummer, feels the chill blockade
Of icebergs stranded at its northern gate.

To thee the echoes of the Island Sound

Answer not vainly, nor in vain the moan
Of the South Breaker prophesying storm.
And thou hast listened, like myself, to men
Sea-periled oft where Anticosti lies
Like a fell spider in its web of fog,
Or where the Grand Bank shallows with the
       wrecks
Of sunken fishers; and to whom strange isles
And frost-rimmed bays and trading stations
       seem
Familiar as Great Neck and Kettle Cove,
Nubble and Boon, the common names of home.

So let me offer thee this lay of mine,
Simple and homely, lacking much thy play
Of color and of fancy. If its theme
And treatment seem to thee befitting youth
Rather than age, let this be my excuse:
It has beguiled some heavy hours and called
Some pleasant memories up; and, better still,
Occasion lent me for a kindly word
To one who is my neighbor and my friend.

THE BAY OF SEVEN ISLANDS.

———•———

THE skipper sailed out of the harbor mouth,
Leaving the apple-bloom of the South
    For the ice of the Eastern seas,
    In his fishing schooner Breeze.

Handsome and brave and young was he,
And the maids of Newbury sighed to see
    His lessening white sail fall
    Under the sea's blue wall.

Through the Northern Gulf and the misty
    screen
Of the isles of Mingan and Madeleine,
    St. Paul's and Blanc Sablon,
    The little Breeze sailed on,

Backward and forward, along the shore
Of lorn and desolate Labrador,
    And found at last her way
    To the Seven Islands Bay.

The little hamlet, nestling below
Great hills white with lingering snow,
    With its tin-roofed chapel stood
    Half hid in the dwarf spruce wood;

Green-turfed, flower-sown, the last outpost
Of summer upon the dreary coast,
    With its gardens small and spare,
    Sad in the frosty air.

Hard by where the skipper's schooner lay,
A fisherman's cottage looked away
    Over isle and bay, and behind
    On mountains dim-defined.

And there twin sisters, fair and young,
Laughed with their stranger guest, and sung

In their native tongue the lays
Of the old Provençal days.

Alike were they, save the faint outline
Of a scar on Suzette's forehead fine;
    And both, it so befell,
    Loved the heretic stranger well.

Both were pleasant to look upon,
But the heart of the skipper clave to one;
    Though less by his eye than heart
    He knew the twain apart.

Despite of alien race and creed,
Well did his wooing of Marguerite speed;
    And the mother's wrath was vain
    As the sister's jealous pain.

The shrill-tongued mistress her house forbade,
And solemn warning was sternly said
    By the black-robed priest, whose word,
    As law the hamlet heard.

But half by voice and half by signs
The skipper said, " A warm sun shines
    On the green-banked Merrimac;
    Wait, watch, till I come back.

"And when you see, from my mast head,
The signal fly of a kerchief red,
    My boat on the shore shall wait;
    Come, when the night is late."

Ah ! weighed with childhood's haunts and
      friends,
And all that the home sky overbends,
    Did ever young love fail
    To turn the trembling scale?

Under the night, on the wet sea sands,
Slowly unclasped their plighted hands:
    One to the cottage hearth,
    And one to his sailor's berth.

What was it the parting lovers heard ?
Nor leaf, nor ripple, nor wing of bird,

But a listener's stealthy tread
On the rock-moss, crisp and dead.

He weighed his anchor, and fished once more
By the black coast-line of Labrador;
    And by love and the north wind driven,
    Sailed back to the Islands Seven.

In the sunset's glow the sisters twain
Saw the Breeze come sailing in again;
    Said Suzette, "Mother dear,
    The heretic's sail is here."

"Go, Marguerite, to your room, and hide;
Your door shall be bolted!" the mother
    cried:
    While Suzette, ill at ease,
    Watched the red sign of the Breeze.

At midnight, down to the waiting skiff
She stole in the shadow of the cliff;
    And out of the Bay's mouth ran
    The schooner with maid and man.

And all night long, on a restless bed,
Her prayers to the Virgin Marguerite said;
 And thought of her lover's pain
 Waiting for her in vain.

Did he pace the sands? Did he pause to hear
The sound of her light step drawing near?
 And, as the slow hours passed,
 Would he doubt her faith at last?

But when she saw through the misty pane,
The morning break on a sea of rain,
 Could even her love avail
 To follow his vanished sail?

Meantime the Breeze, with favoring wind,
Left the rugged Moisic hills behind,
 And heard from an unseen shore
 The falls of Manitou roar.

On the morrow's morn, in the thick, gray
  weather
They sat on the reeling deck together,

Lover and counterfeit,
Of hapless Marguerite.

With a lover's hand, from her forehead fair
He smoothed away her jet-black hair.
What was it his fond eyes met?
The scar of the false Suzette!

Fiercely he shouted: "Bear away
East by north for Seven Isles Bay!"
The maiden wept and prayed,
But the ship her helm obeyed.

Once more the Bay of the Isles they found:
They heard the bell of the chapel sound,
And the chant of the dying sung
In the harsh, wild Indian tongue.

A feeling of mystery, change, and awe
Was in all they heard and all they saw:
Spell-bound the hamlet lay
In the hush of its lonely bay.

2

And when they came to the cottage door,
The mother rose up from her weeping sore,
    And with angry gestures met
    The scared look of Suzette.

"Here is your daughter," the skipper said ;
"Give me the one I love instead."
    But the woman sternly spake ;
    "Go, see if the dead will wake!"

He looked.   Her sweet face still and white
And strange in the noonday taper light,
    She lay on her little bed,
    With the cross at her feet and head.

In a passion of grief the strong man bent
Down to her face, and, kissing it, went
    Back to the waiting Breeze,
    Back to the mournful seas.

Never again to the Merrimac
And Newbury's homes that bark came back.

Whether her fate she met
On the shores of Carraquette,

Miscou, or Tracadie, who can say?
But even yet at Seven Isles Bay
    Is told the ghostly tale
    Of a weird, unspoken sail,

In the pale, sad light of the Northern day
Seen by the blanketed Montagnais,
    Or squaw, in her small kyack,
    Crossing the spectre's track.

On the deck a maiden wrings her hands ;
Her likeness kneels on the gray coast sands ;
    One in her wild despair,
    And one in the trance of prayer.

She flits before no earthly blast,
The red sign fluttering from her mast,
    Over the solemn seas,
    The ghost of the schooner Breeze !

HOW THE WOMEN WENT FROM DOVER.
1662.

THE tossing spray of Cocheco's fall
Hardened to ice on its rocky wall,
As through Dover town, in the chill, gray
        dawn,
Three women passed, at the cart-tail drawn![1]

[1] The following is a copy of the warrant issued by Major Waldron, of Dover, in 1662. The Quakers, as was their wont, prophesied against him, and saw, as they supposed, the fulfillment of their prophecy when, many years after, he was killed by the Indians.

To the constables of Dover, Hampton, Salisbury, Newbury, Rowley, Ipswich, Wenham, Lynn, Boston, Roxbury, Dedham, and until these vagabond Quakers are carried out of this jurisdiction.

You, and every one of you, are required, in the King's Majesty's name, to take these vagabond Quakers, Anne Colman, Mary Tomkins, and Alice Ambrose, and make them fast to the cart's tail, and driving the cart through

Bared to the waist for the north wind's grip
And keener sting of the constable's whip,
The blood that followed each hissing blow
Froze as it sprinkled the winter snow.

Priest and ruler, boy and maid
Followed the dismal cavalcade;
And from door and window, open thrown,
Looked and wondered gaffer and crone.

your several towns, to whip them upon their naked
backs not exceeding ten stripes apiece on each of them
in each town; and so to convey them from constable
to constable till they are out of this jurisdiction, as you
will answer it at your peril; and this shall be your warrant.   RICHARD WALDRON.
   Dated at Dover, December 22, 1662.

   This warrant was executed only in Dover and Hampton. At Salisbury the constable refused to obey it. He
was sustained by the town's people, who were under the
influence of Major Robert Pike, the leading man in the
lower valley of the Merrimac, who stood far in advance
of his time, as an advocate of religious freedom, and an
opponent of ecclesiastical authority. He had the moral
courage to address an able and manly letter to the court at
Salem, remonstrating against the witchcraft trials.

"God is our witness," the victims cried,
"We suffer for Him who for all men died:
The wrong ye do has been done before,
We bear the stripes that the Master bore

"And thou, O Richard Waldron, for whom
We hear the feet of a coming doom,
On thy cruel heart and thy hand of wrong
Vengeance is sure, though it tarry long.

"In the light of the Lord, a flame we see
Climb and kindle a proud roof-tree;
And beneath it an old man lying dead,
With stains of blood on his hoary head."

"Smite, Goodman Hate-Evil! — harder still!"
The magistrate cried, "lay on with a will!
Drive out of their bodies the Father of Lies,
Who through them preaches and prophesies!"

So into the forest they held their way,
By winding river and frost-rimmed bay,

Over wind-swept hills that felt the beat
Of the winter sea at their icy feet.

The Indian hunter, searching his traps,
Peered stealthily through the forest gaps;
And the outlying settler shook his head, —
" They 're witches going to jail," he said.   .

At last a meeting-house came in view;
A blast on his horn the constable blew;
And the boys of Hampton cried up and down,
" The Quakers have come!" to the wondering
     town.

From barn and woodpile the goodman came;
The goodwife quitted her quilting frame,
With her child at her breast; and, hobbling
     slow,
The grandam followed to see the show.

Once more the torturing whip was swung,
Once more keen lashes the bare flesh stung.

"Oh, spare! they are bleeding!" a little maid
    cried,
And covered her face the sight to hide.

A murmur ran round the crowd : "Good folks,"
Quoth the constable, busy counting the strokes,
"No pity to wretches like these is due,
They have beaten the gospel black and blue!"

Then a pallid woman, in wild-eyed fear,
With her wooden noggin of milk drew near.
"Drink, poor hearts!" A rude hand smote
Her draught away from a parching throat.

"Take heed," one whispered, "they'll take
    your cow
For fines, as they took your horse and plow,
And the bed from under you." "Even so,"
She said. "They are cruel as death I know."

Then on they passed, in the waning day,
Through Seabrook woods, a weariful way;

By great salt meadows and sand-hills bare,
And glimpses of blue sea here and there.

By the meeting-house in Salisbury town,
The sufferers stood, in the red sundown,
Bare for the lash! O pitying Night,
Drop swift thy curtain and hide the sight!

With shame in his eye and wrath on his lip
The Salisbury constable dropped his whip.
"This warrant means murder foul and red;
Cursed is he who serves it," he said.

"Show me the order, and meanwhile strike
A blow at your peril!" said Justice Pike.
Of all the rulers the land possessed,
Wisest and boldest was he, and best.

He scoffed at witchcraft; the priest he met
As man meets man; his feet he set
Beyond his dark age, standing upright,
Soul-free, with his face to the morning light.

He read the warrant: " *These convey*
From our precincts ; at every town on the
     way
Give each ten lashes." " God judge the brute !
I tread his order under my foot!

" Cut loose these poor ones and let them
     go ;
Come what will of it, all men shall know
No warrant is good, though backed by the
     Crown,
For whipping women in Salisbury town!"

The hearts of the villagers, half released
From creed of terror and rule of priest,
By a primal instinct owned the right
Of human pity in law's despite.

For ruth and chivalry only slept,
His Saxon manhood the yeoman kept;
Quicker or slower, the same blood ran
In the Cavalier and the Puritan.

The Quakers sank on their knees in praise
And thanks. A last, low sunset blaze
Flashed out from under a cloud, and shed
A golden glory on each bowed head.

The tale is one of an evil time,
When souls were fettered and thought was
      crime,
And heresy's whisper above its breath
Meant shameful scourging and bonds and
      death!

What marvel that, hunted and sorely tried,
Even woman rebuked and prophesied,
And soft words rarely answered back
The grim persuasion of whip and rack!

If her cry from the whipping-post and
      jail
Pierced sharp as the Kenite's driven nail,
O woman, at ease in these happier days,
Forbear to judge of thy sister's ways!

How much thy beautiful life may owe
To her faith and courage thou canst not
    know,
Nor how from the paths of thy calm retreat
She smoothed the thorns with her bleeding
    feet.

A SUMMER PILGRIMAGE.

To kneel before some saintly shrine,
To breathe the health of airs divine,
Or bathe where sacred rivers flow,
The cowled and turbaned pilgrims go.
I too, a palmer, take, as they,
With staff and scallop-shell my way,
To feel, from burdening cares and ills,
The strong uplifting of the hills.

The years are many since, at first,
For dreamed-of wonders all athirst,
I saw on Winnepesaukee fall
The shadow of the mountain wall.
Ah! where are they who sailed with me
The beautiful island-studded sea?
And am I he whose keen surprise
Flashed out from such unclouded eyes?

Still, when the sun of summer burns,
My longing for the hills returns;
And northward, leaving at my back
The warm vale of the Merrimac,
I go to meet the winds of morn,
Blown down the hill-gaps, mountain-born,
Breathe scent of pines, and satisfy
The hunger of a lowland eye.

Again I see the day decline
Along the ridged horizon line;
Touching the hill-tops, as a nun
Her beaded rosary, sinks the sun.
One lake lies golden, which shall soon
Be silver in the rising moon;
And one the crimson of the skies
And mountain purple multiplies.

With the untroubled quiet blends
The distance-softened voice of friends;
The girl's light laugh no discord brings
To the low song the pine-tree sings;

And, not unwelcome, comes the hail
Of boyhood from his nearing sail.
The human presence breaks no spell,
And sunset still is miracle!

Calm as the hour, methinks I feel
A sense of worship o'er me steal;
Not that of satyr-charming Pan,
No cult of Nature shaming man,
Not Beauty's self, but that which lives
And shines through all the veils it weaves, —
Soul of the mountain, lake, and wood,
Their witness to the Eternal Good!

And if, by fond illusion, here
The earth to heaven seems drawing near,
And yon outlying range invites
To other and serener heights,
Scarce hid behind its topmost swell,
The shining Mounts Delectable!
A dream may hint of truth no less
Than the sharp light of wakefulness.

As through her veil of incense smoke
Of old the spell-rapt priestess spoke,
More than her heathen oracle,
May not this trance of sunset tell
That Nature's forms of loveliness
Their heavenly archetypes confess,
Fashioned like Israel's ark alone
From patterns in the Mount made known?

A holier beauty overbroods
These fair and faint similitudes;
Yet not unblest is he who sees
Shadows of God's realities,
And knows beyond this masquerade
Of shape and color, light and shade,
And dawn and set, and wax and wane,
Eternal verities remain.

O gems of sapphire, granite set!
O hills that charmed horizons fret!
I know how fair your morns can break,
In rosy light on isle and lake;

How over wooded slopes can run
The noonday play of cloud and sun,
And evening droop her oriflamme
Of gold and red in still Asquam.

The summer moons may round again,
And careless feet these hills profane;
These sunsets waste on vacant eyes
The lavish splendor of the skies;
Fashion and folly, misplaced here,
Sigh for their natural atmosphere,
And traveled pride the outlook scorn
Of lesser heights than Matterhorn:

But let me dream that hill and sky
Of unseen beauty prophesy;
And in these tinted lakes behold
The trailing of the raiment fold
Of that which, still eluding gaze,
Allures to upward-tending ways,
Whose footprints make, wherever found,
Our common earth a holy ground.

3

THE ROCK-TOMB OF BRADORE.

A DREAR and desolate shore!
Where no tree unfolds its leaves,
And never the spring wind weaves
Green grass for the hunter's tread;
A land forsaken and dead,
Where the ghostly icebergs go
And come with the ebb and flow
   Of the waters of Bradore!

A wanderer, from a land
By summer breezes fanned,
Looked round him, awed, subdued,
By the dreadful solitude,
Hearing alone the cry
Of sea-birds clanging by,
The crash and grind of the floe,

Wail of wind and wash of tide.
"O wretched land!" he cried,
"Land of all lands the worst,
  God forsaken and curst!
Thy gates of rock should show
    The words the Tuscan seer
Read in the Realm of Woe:
    Hope entereth not here!"

Lo! at his feet there stood
A block of smooth larch wood,
Waif of some wandering wave,
Beside a rock-closed cave
By Nature fashioned for a grave,
Safe from the ravening bear
And fierce fowl of the air,
Wherein to rest was laid
A twenty summers' maid,
Whose blood had equal share
Of the lands of vine and snow,
Half French, half Eskimo.
In letters uneffaced,
Upon the block were traced

The grief and hope of man,
And thus the legend ran:
    "*We loved her!*
Words cannot tell how well!
    We loved her!
    God loved her!
And called her home to peace and rest.
    We love her!"

The stranger paused and read.
"O winter land!" he said,
"Thy right to be I own;
God leaves thee not alone.
And if thy fierce winds blow
Over drear wastes of rock and snow,
And at thy iron gates
The ghostly iceberg waits,
    Thy homes and hearts are dear.
Thy sorrow o'er thy sacred dust
Is sanctified by hope and trust;
    God's love and man's are here.

And love where'er it goes
Makes its own atmosphere;
Its flowers of Paradise
Take root in the eternal ice,
   And bloom through Polar snows!"

STORM ON LAKE ASQUAM.

A CLOUD, like that the old-time Hebrew saw
  On Carmel prophesying rain, began
  To lift itself o'er wooded Cardigan,
Growing and blackening. Suddenly, a flaw

Of chill wind menaced ; then a strong blast beat
  Down the long valley's murmuring pines, and
      woke
  The noon-dream of the sleeping lake, and broke
Its smooth steel mirror at the mountains' feet.

Thunderous and vast, a fire-veined darkness
      swept
  Over the rough pine-bearded Asquam range ;
  A wraith of tempest, wonderful and strange,
From peak to peak the cloudy giant stepped.

One moment, as if challenging the storm,
   Chocorua's tall, defiant sentinel
   Looked from his watch - tower; then the
      shadow fell,
And the wild rain-drift blotted out his form.

And over all the still unhidden sun,
   Weaving its light through slant-blown veils
      of rain,
   Smiled on the trouble, as hope smiles on pain ;
And, when the tumult and the strife were done,

With one foot on the lake and one on land,
   Framing within his crescent's tinted streak
   A far-off picture of the Melvin peak,
Spent broken clouds the rainbow's angel
      spanned.

THE WISHING BRIDGE.

AMONG the legends sung or said
  Along our rocky shore,
The Wishing Bridge of Marblehead
  May well be sung once more.

An hundred years ago (so ran
  The old-time story) all
Good wishes said above its span
  Would, soon or late, befall.

If pure and earnest, never failed
  The prayers of man or maid
For him who on the deep sea sailed,
  For her at home who stayed.

Once thither came two girls from school,
   And wished in childish glee:
And one would be a queen and rule,
   And one the world would see.

Time passed; with change of hopes and fears,
   And in the self-same place,
Two women, gray with middle years,
   Stood, wondering, face to face.

With wakened memories, as they met,
   They queried what had been:
" A poor man's wife am I, and yet,"
   Said one, " I am a queen.

" My realm a little homestead is,
   Where, lacking crown and throne,
I rule by loving services
   And patient toil alone."

The other said: " The great world lies
   Beyond me as it laid;

O'er love's and duty's boundaries
   My feet have never strayed.

"I see but common sights of home,
   Its common sounds I hear,
My widowed mother's sick-bed room
   Sufficeth for my sphere.

"I read to her some pleasant page
   Of travel far and wide,
And in a dreamy pilgrimage
   We wander side by side.

"And when, at last, she falls asleep,
   My book becomes to me
A magic glass: my watch I keep,
   But all the world I see.

"A farm-wife queen your place you fill,
   While fancy's privilege
Is mine to walk the earth at will,
   Thanks to the Wishing Bridge."

"Nay, leave the legend for the truth,"
    The other cried, "and say
God gives the wishes of our youth
    But in His own best way!"

THE MYSTIC'S CHRISTMAS.

"ALL hail!" the bells of Christmas rang,
"All hail!" the monks at Christmas sang,
  The merry monks who kept with cheer
  The gladdest day of all their year.

  But still apart, unmoved thereat,
  A pious elder brother sat
  Silent, in his accustomed place,
  With God's sweet peace upon his face.

"Why sitt'st thou thus?" his brethren cried.
"It is the blessed Christmas-tide;
  The Christmas lights are all aglow,
  The sacred lilies bud and blow.

"Above our heads the joy-bells ring,
  Without the happy children sing,

And all God's creatures hail the morn
On which the holy Christ was born!

"Rejoice with us; no more rebuke
Our gladness with thy quiet look."
The gray monk answered: "Keep, I pray,
Even as ye list, the Lord's birthday.

"Let heathen Yule fires flicker red
Where thronged refectory feasts are spread;
With mystery-play and masque and mime
And wait-songs speed the holy time!

"The blindest faith may haply save;
The Lord accepts the things we have;
And reverence, howsoe'er it strays,
May find at last the shining ways.

"They needs must grope who cannot see,
The blade before the ear must be;
As ye are feeling I have felt,
And where ye dwell I too have dwelt.

" But now, beyond the things of sense,
  Beyond occasions and events,
  I know, through God's exceeding grace,
  Release from form and time and place.

" I listen, from no mortal tongue,
  To hear the song the angels sung;
  And wait within myself to know
  The Christmas lilies bud and blow.

" The outward symbols disappear
  From him whose inward sight is clear;
  And small must be the choice of days
  To him who fills them all with praise!

" Keep while you need it, brothers mine,
  With honest zeal your Christmas sign,
  But judge not him who every morn
  Feels in his heart the Lord Christ born! "

WHAT THE TRAVELER SAID AT SUNSET.

THE shadows grow and deepen round me,
　I feel the dew-fall in the air;
The muezzin of the darkening thicket
　I hear the night-thrush call to prayer.

The evening wind is sad with farewells,
　And loving hands unclasp from mine;
Alone I go to meet the darkness
　Across an awful boundary-line.

As from the lighted hearths behind me
　I pass with slow, reluctant feet,
What waits me in the land of strangeness?
　What face shall smile, what voice shall greet?

What space shall awe, what brightness blind
　　me?
What thunder-roll of music stun?

What vast processions sweep before me
    Of shapes unknown beneath the sun?

I shrink from unaccustomed glory,
    I dread the myriad-voicéd strain;
Give me the unforgotten faces,
    And let my lost ones speak again.

He will not chide my mortal yearning
    Who is our Brother and our Friend;
In whose full life, divine and human,
    The heavenly and the earthly blend.

Mine be the joy of soul-communion,
    The sense of spiritual strength renewed,
The reverence for the pure and holy,
    The dear delight of doing good.

No fitting ear is mine to listen
    An endless anthem's rise and fall;
No curious eye is mine to measure
    The pearl gate and the jasper wall.

For love must needs be more than knowledge:
  What matter if I never know
Why Aldebaran's star is ruddy
  Or warmer Sirius white as snow!

Forgive my human words, O Father!
  I go Thy larger truth to prove;
Thy mercy shall transcend my longing:
  I seek but love, and Thou art Love!

I go to find my lost and mourned for
  Safe in Thy sheltering goodness still,
And all that hope and faith foreshadow
  Made perfect in Thy holy will!

4

A GREETING.

HARRIET BEECHER STOWE'S SEVENTIETH ANNIVERSARY, 1882.

THRICE welcome from the Land of Flowers
And golden-fruited orange bowers
To this sweet, green-turfed June of ours!
To her who, in our evil time,
Dragged into light the nation's crime
With strength beyond the strength of men,
And, mightier than their swords, her pen!
To her who world-wide entrance gave
To the log-cabin of the slave;
Made all his wrongs and sorrows known,
And all earth's languages his own, —
North, South, and East and West, made all
The common air electrical,
Until the o'ercharged bolts of heaven
Blazed down, and every chain was riven!

Welcome from each and all to her
Whose Wooing of the Minister
Revealed the warm heart of the man
Beneath the creed-bound Puritan,
And taught the kinship of the love
Of man below and God above;
To her whose vigorous pencil-strokes
Sketched into life her Oldtown Folks, —
Whose fireside stories, grave or gay,
In quaint Sam Lawson's vagrant way,
With old New England's flavor rife,
Waifs from her rude idyllic life,
Are racy as the legends old
By Chaucer or Boccaccio told;
To her who keeps, through change of place
And time, her native strength and grace,
Alike where warm Sorrento smiles,
Or where, by birchen-shaded isles,
Whose summer winds have shivered o'er
The icy drift of Labrador,
She lifts to light the priceless Pearl
Of Harpswell's angel-beckoned girl!

To her at threescore years and ten
Be tributes of the tongue and pen;
Be honor, praise, and heart-thanks given,
The loves of earth, the hopes of heaven!

Ah, dearer than the praise that stirs
The air to-day, our love is hers!
She needs no guaranty of fame
Whose own is linked with Freedom's name.
Long ages after ours shall keep
Her memory living while we sleep;
The waves that wash our gray coast lines,
The winds that rock the Southern pines,
Shall sing of her; the unending years
Shall tell her tale in unborn ears.
And when, with sins and follies past,
Are numbered color-hate and caste,
White, black, and red shall own as one
The noblest work by woman done.

WILSON.[1]

THE lowliest born of all the land,
He wrung from Fate's reluctant hand
   The gifts which happier boyhood claims;
And, tasting on a thankless soil
The bitter bread of unpaid toil,
   He fed his soul with noble aims.

And Nature, kindly provident,
To him the future's promise lent;
   The powers that shape man's destinies,
Patience and faith and toil, he knew;
The close horizon round him grew,
   Broad with great possibilities.

[1] Read at the Massachusetts Club on the seventieth anniversary of the birthday of Vice-President Wilson.

By the low hearth-fire's fitful blaze
He read of old heroic days,
　　The sage's thought, the patriot's speech;
Unhelped, alone, himself he taught,
His school the craft at which he wrought,
　　His lore the book within his reach.

He felt his country's need; he knew
The work her children had to do;
　　And when, at last, he heard the call
In her behalf to serve and dare,
Beside his senatorial chair
　　He stood the unquestioned peer of all.

Beyond the accident of birth
He proved his simple manhood's worth;
　　Ancestral pride and classic grace
Confessed the large-brained artisan,
So clear of sight, so wise in plan
　　And counsel, equal to his place.

With glance intuitive he saw
Through all disguise of form and law,

And read men like an open book;
Fearless and firm, he never quailed
Nor turned aside for threats, nor failed
　To do the thing he undertook.

How wise, how brave, he was, how well
He bore himself, let history tell
　While waves our flag o'er land and sea,
No black thread in its warp or weft;
He found dissevered States, he left
　A grateful Nation, strong and free!

IN MEMORY.

J. T. F.

As a guest who may not stay
Long and sad farewells to say
Glides with smiling face away,

Of the sweetness and the zest
Of thy happy life possessed
Thou hast left us at thy best.

Warm of heart and clear of brain,
Of thy sun-bright spirit's wane
Thou hast spared us all the pain.

Now that thou hast gone away,
What is left of one to say
Who was open as the day?

What is there to gloss or shun?
Save with kindly voices none
Speak thy name beneath the sun.

Safe thou art on every side,
Friendship nothing finds to hide,
Love's demand is satisfied.

Over manly strength and worth,
At thy desk of toil, or hearth,
Played the lambent light of mirth, —

Mirth that lit, but never burned;
All thy blame to pity turned;
Hatred thou hadst never learned.

Every harsh and vexing thing
At thy home-fire lost its sting;
Where thou wast was always spring.

And thy perfect trust in good,
Faith in man and womanhood,
Chance and change and time withstood.

Small respect for cant and whine,
Bigot's zeal and hate malign,
Had that sunny soul of thine.

But to thee was duty's claim
Sacred, and thy lips became
Reverent with one holy Name.

Therefore, on thy unknown way,
Go in God's peace! We who stay
But a little while delay.

Keep for us, O friend, where'er
Thou art waiting, all that here
Made thy earthly presence dear;

Something of thy pleasant past
On a ground of wonder cast,
In the stiller waters glassed!

Keep the human heart of thee;
Let the mortal only be
Clothed in immortality.

And when fall our feet as fell
Thine upon the asphodel,
Let thy old smile greet us well;

Proving in a world of bliss
What we fondly dream in this, —
Love is one with holiness!

THE POET AND THE CHILDREN.

H. W. L.

With a glory of winter sunshine
  Over his locks of gray,
In the old historic mansion
  He sat on his last birthday;

With his books and his pleasant pictures,
  And his household and his kin,
While a sound as of myriads singing
  From far and near stole in.

It came from his own fair city,
  From the prairie's boundless plain,
From the Golden Gate of sunset,
  And the cedarn woods of Maine.

And his heart grew warm within him,
　And his moistening eyes grew dim,
For he knew that his country's children
　Were singing the songs of him :

The lays of his life's glad morning,
　The psalms of his evening time,
Whose echoes shall float forever
　On the winds of every clime.

All their beautiful consolations,
　Sent forth like birds of cheer,
Came flocking back to his windows,
　And sang in the Poet's ear.

Grateful, but solemn and tender,
　The music rose and fell
With a joy akin to sadness
　And a greeting like farewell.

With a sense of awe he listened
　To the voices sweet and young ;

The last of earth and the first of heaven
  Seemed in the songs they sung.

And waiting a little longer
  For the wonderful change to come,
He heard the Summoning Angel,
  Who calls God's children home!

And to him in a holier welcome
  Was the mystical meaning given
Of the words of the blessed Master:
  "Of such is the kingdom of heaven!"

RABBI ISHMAEL.

THE Rabbi Ishmael, with the woe and sin
Of the world heavy upon him, entering in
The Holy of Holies, saw an awful Face
With terrible splendor filling all the place.
"O Ishmael Ben Elisha!" said a voice,
"What seekest thou? What blessing is thy
       choice?"
And, knowing that he stood before the Lord,
Within the shadow of the cherubim,
Wide-winged between the blinding light and
       him,
He bowed himself, and uttered not a word,
But in the silence of his soul was prayer:
"O thou Eternal! I am one of all,
And nothing ask that others may not share.
Thou art almighty; we are weak and small,
And yet thy children: let thy mercy spare!"

Trembling, he raised his eyes, and in the place
Of the insufferable glory, lo! a face
Of more than mortal tenderness, that bent
Graciously down in token of assent,
And, smiling, vanished!   With strange joy elate,
The wondering Rabbi sought the temple's gate.
Radiant as Moses from the Mount, he stood
And cried aloud unto the multitude:
"O Israel, hear!   The Lord our God is good!
Mine eyes have seen his glory and his grace;
Beyond his judgments shall his love endure;
The mercy of the All Merciful is sure!"

VALUATION.

THE old Squire said, as he stood by his gate,
    And his neighbor, the Deacon, went by,
" In spite of my bank stock and real estate,
    You are better off, Deacon, than I.

" We're both growing old, and the end's draw-
        ing near,
    You have less of this world to resign,
But in Heaven's appraisal your assets, I fear,
    Will reckon up greater than mine.

"They say I am rich, but I'm feeling so poor,
    I wish I could swap with you even:
The pounds I have lived for and laid up in
        store
    For the shillings and pence you have given."

5

" Well, Squire," said the Deacon, with shrewd
        common sense,
    While his eye had a twinkle of fun,
" Let your pounds take the way of my shillings
        and pence,
    And the thing can be easily done !"

WINTER ROSES.[1]

My garden roses long ago
   Have perished from the leaf-strewn walks;
Their pale, fair sisters smile no more
   Upon the sweet-brier stalks.

Gone with the flower-time of my life,
   Spring's violets, summer's blooming pride,
And Nature's winter and my own
   Stand, flowerless, side by side.

So might I yesterday have sung;
   To-day, in bleak December's noon,
Come sweetest fragrance, shapes, and hues,
   The rosy wealth of June!

Bless the young hands that culled the gift,
   And bless the hearts that prompted it;

[1] In reply to a flower gift from Mrs. Putnam's school at Jamaica Plain.

If undeserved it comes, at least
  It seems not all unfit.

Of old my Quaker ancestors
  Had gifts of forty stripes save one;
To-day as many roses crown
  The gray head of their son.

And with them, to my fancy's eye,
  The fresh-faced givers smiling come,
And nine and thirty happy girls
  Make glad a lonely room.

They bring the atmosphere of youth;
  The light and warmth of long ago
Are in my heart, and on my cheek
  The airs of morning blow.

O buds of girlhood, yet unblown,
  And fairer than the gift ye chose,
For you may years like leaves unfold
  The heart of Sharon's rose!

HYMN.

(FOR THE AMERICAN HORTICULTURAL SOCIETY.)

1882.

O PAINTER of the fruits and flowers,
   We own Thy wise design,
Whereby these human hands of ours
   May share the work of Thine!

Apart from Thee we plant in vain
   The root and sow the seed;
Thy early and Thy later rain,
   Thy sun and dew we need.

Our toil is sweet with thankfulness,
   Our burden is our boon;
The curse of Earth's gray morning is
   The blessing of its noon.

Why search the wide world everywhere
    For Eden's unknown ground? —
That garden of the primal pair
    May nevermore be found.

But, blest by Thee, our patient toil
    May right the ancient wrong,
And give to every clime and soil
    The beauty lost so long.

Our homestead flowers and fruited trees
    May Eden's orchard shame;
We taste the tempting sweets of these
    Like Eve, without her blame.

And, North and South and East and West
    The pride of every zone,
The fairest, rarest and the best
    May all be made our own.

Its earliest shrines the young world sought
    In hill-groves and in bowers,

The fittest offerings thither brought
 Were Thy own fruits and flowers.

And still with reverent hands we cull
 Thy gifts each year renewed;
The good is always beautiful,
 The beautiful is good.

GODSPEED.

OUTBOUND, your bark awaits you. Were I
    one
  Whose prayer availeth much, my wish should
    be
  Your favoring trade-wind and consenting sea.
By sail or steed was never love outrun,
And, here or there, love follows her in whom
  All graces and sweet charities unite,
    The old Greek beauty set in holier light;
And her for whom New England's byways
    bloom,
Who walks among us welcome as the Spring,
  Calling up blossoms where her light feet
    stray.
  God keep you both, make beautiful your
    way,
Comfort, console, and bless; and safely bring,
Ere yet I make upon a vaster sea
The unreturning voyage, my friends to me.

AT LAST.

When on my day of life the night is falling,
  And, in the winds from unsunned spaces
      blown,
I hear far voices out of darkness calling
  My feet to paths unknown,

Thou who hast made my home of life so
    pleasant,
  Leave not its tenant when its walls decay;
O Love Divine, O Helper ever present,
  Be Thou my strength and stay!

Be near me when all else is from me drifting:
  Earth, sky, home's pictures, days of shade
      and shine,
And kindly faces to my own uplifting
  The love which answers mine.

I have but Thee, my Father! let Thy spirit
　　Be with me then to comfort and uphold;
No gate of pearl, no branch of palm I merit,
　　Nor street of shining gold.

Suffice it if—my good and ill unreckoned,
　　And both forgiven through thy abounding
　　　　grace —
I find myself by hands familiar beckoned
　　Unto my fitting place.

Some humble door among Thy many mansions,
　　Some sheltering shade where sin and striving
　　　　cease,
And flows forever through heaven's green ex-
　　pansions
　　The river of Thy peace.

There, from the music round about me stealing,
　　I fain would learn the new and holy song,
And find at last, beneath Thy trees of healing,
　　The life for which I long.

OUR COUNTRY.

READ AT WOODSTOCK, CONN., JULY 4, 1883.

WE give thy natal day to hope,
  O Country of our love and prayer!
Thy way is down no fatal slope,
  But up to freer sun and air.

Tried as by furnace-fires, and yet
  By God's grace only stronger made,
In future task before thee set
  Thou shalt not lack the old-time aid.

The fathers sleep, but men remain
  As wise, as true, and brave as they;
Why count the loss and not the gain? —
  The best is that we have to-day.

Whatc'er of folly, shame, or crime,
  Within thy mighty bounds transpires,
With speed defying space and time
  Comes to us on the accusing wires;

While of thy wealth of noble deeds,
  Thy homes of peace, thy votes unsold,
The love that pleads for human needs,
  The wrong redressed, but half is told!

We read each felon's chronicle,
  His acts, his words, his gallows-mood;
We know the single sinner well
  And not the nine and ninety good.

Yet if, on daily scandals fed,
  We seem at times to doubt thy worth,
We know thee still, when all is said,
  The best and dearest spot on earth.

From the warm Mexic Gulf, or where
  Belted with flowers Los Angeles

Basks in the semi-tropic air,
  To where Katahdin's cedar trees

Are dwarfed and bent by Northern winds,
  Thy plenty's horn is yearly filled;
Alone, the rounding century finds
  Thy liberal soil by free hands tilled.

A refuge for the wronged and poor,
  Thy generous heart has borne the blame
That, with them, through thy open door,
  The old world's evil outcasts came.

But, with thy just and equal rule,
  And labor's need and breadth of lands,
Free press and rostrum, church and school,
  Thy sure, if slow, transforming hands

Shall mould even them to thy design,
  Making a blessing of the ban;
And Freedom's chemistry combine
  The alien elements of man.

The power that broke their prison bar
　　And set the dusky millions free,
And welded in the flame of war
　　The Union fast to Liberty,

Shall it not deal with other ills,
　　Redress the red man's grievance, break
The Circean cup which shames and kills,
　　And Labor full requital make?

Alone to such as fitly bear
　　Thy civic honors bid them fall?
And call thy daughters forth to share
　　The rights and duties pledged to all?

Give every child his right of school,
　　Merge private greed in public good,
And spare a treasury overfull
　　The tax upon a poor man's food?

No lack was in thy primal stock,
　　No weakling founders builded here;

Thine were the men of Plymouth Rock,
　The Huguenot and Cavalier;

And they whose firm endurance gained
　The freedom of the souls of men,
Whose hands, unstained with blood, main-
　　tained
　The swordless commonwealth of Penn.

And thine shall be the power of all
　To do the work which duty bids.
And make the people's council hall
　As lasting as the Pyramids!

Well have thy later years made good
　Thy brave-said word a century back,
The pledge of human brotherhood,
　The equal claim of white and black.

That word still echoes round the world,
　And all who hear it turn to thee,
And read upon thy flag unfurled
　The prophecies of destiny.

Thy great world-lesson all shall learn,
  The nations in thy school shall sit,
Earth's farthest mountain-tops shall burn
  With watch-fires from thy own uplit.

Great without seeking to be great
  By fraud or conquest, rich in gold,
But richer in the large estate
  Of virtue which thy children hold,

With peace that comes of purity
  And strength to simple justice due,
So runs our loyal dream of thee;
  God of our fathers! — make it true.

O Land of lands! to thee we give
  Our prayers, our hopes, our service free;
For thee thy sons shall nobly live,
  And at thy need shall die for thee!

THE "STORY OF IDA."

WEARY of jangling noises never stilled,
   The skeptic's sneer, the bigot's hate, the din
   Of clashing texts, the webs of creed men spin
Round simple truth, the children grown who build
With gilded cards their new Jerusalem,
   Busy, with sacerdotal tailorings
   And tinsel gauds, bedizening holy things, ·
I turn, with glad and grateful heart, from them
To the sweet story of the Florentine
   Immortal in her blameless maidenhood,
   Beautiful as God's angels and as good;
Feeling that life, even now, may be divine
With love no wrong can ever change to hate,
No sin make less than all-compassionate!

AN AUTOGRAPH.

I WRITE my name as one,
On sands by waves o'errun
Or winter's frosted pane,
Traces a record vain.

Oblivion's blankness claims
Wiser and better names,
And well my own may pass
As from the strand or glass.

Wash on, O waves of time!
Melt, noons, the frosty rime!
Welcome the shadow vast,
The silence that shall last!

When I and all who know
And love me vanish so,

What harm to them or me
Will the lost memory be?

If any words of mine,
Through right of life divine,
Remain, what matters it
Whose hand the message writ?

Why should the " crowner's quest "
Sit on my worst or best?
Why should the showman claim
The poor ghost of my name?

Yet, as when dies a sound
Its spectre lingers round,
Haply my spent life will
Leave some faint echo still.

A whisper giving breath
Of praise or blame to death,
Soothing or saddening such
As loved the living much.

Therefore with yearnings vain
And fond I still would fain
A kindly judgment seek,
A tender thought bespeak.

And, while my words are read,
Let this at least be said:
" Whate'er his life's defeatures,
He loved his fellow creatures.

"If, of the Law's stone table,
To hold he scarce was able
The first great precept fast,
He kept for man the last.

" Through mortal lapse and dullness
What lacks the Eternal Fullness,
If still our weakness can
Love Him in loving man?

" Age brought him no despairing
Of the world's future faring;

In human nature still
He found more good than ill.

" To all who dumbly suffered,
　His tongue and pen he offered;
　His life was not his own,
　Nor lived for self alone.

" Hater of din and riot
　He lived in days unquiet;
　And, lover of all beauty,
　Trod the hard ways of duty.

" He meant no wrong to any
　He sought the good of many,
　Yet knew both sin and folly, —
　May God forgive him wholly ! "

Standard and Popular Library Books

SELECTED FROM THE CATALOGUE OF

HOUGHTON, MIFFLIN AND COMPANY.

JOHN ADAMS and Abigail Adams.
Familiar Letters of, during the Revolution. 12mo, $2.00.

Louis Agassiz.
Methods of Study in Natural History. Illus. 16mo, $1.50.
Geological Sketches. First Series. 16mo, $1.50.
Geological Sketches. Second Series. 16mo, $1.50.
A Journey in Brazil. Illustrated. 8vo, $5.00.

Thomas Bailey Aldrich.
Story of a Bad Boy. Illustrated. 12mo, $1.50.
Marjorie Daw and Other People. 12mo, $1.50.
Prudence Palfrey. 12mo, $1.50.
The Queen of Sheba. 16mo, $1.50.
The Stillwater Tragedy. 12mo, $1.50.
From Ponkapog to Pesth. 16mo, $1.25.
Cloth of Gold and Other Poems. 12mo, $1.50.
Flower and Thorn. Later Poems. 16mo, $1.25.
Poems, Complete. Illustrated. 8vo, $5.00.
Mercedes, and Later Lyrics. 12mo.

American Commonwealths.
Edited by HORACE E. SCUDDER.
Virginia. By John Esten Cooke.
Oregon. By William Barrows.
(In Preparation.)
South Carolina. By Hon. W. H. Trescot.
Kentucky. By N. S. Shaler.
Maryland. By Wm. Hand Browne.
Pennsylvania. By Hon. Wayne MacVeagh.
Each volume, 16mo, $1.25.
Others to be announced hereafter.

American Men of Letters.

Edited by CHARLES DUDLEY WARNER.
Washington Irving. By Charles Dudley Warner.
Noah Webster. By Horace E. Scudder.
Henry D. Thoreau. By Frank B. Sanborn.
George Ripley. By O. B. Frothingham.
J. Fenimore Cooper. By Prof. T. R. Lounsbury.
(*In Preparation.*)
Ralph Waldo Emerson. By Oliver Wendell Holmes.
Nathaniel Hawthorne. By James Russell Lowell.
Margaret Fuller. By T. W. Higginson.
Edmund Quincy. By Sidney Howard Gay.
William Cullen Bryant. By John Bigelow.
Bayard Taylor. By J. R. G. Hassard.
William Gilmore Simms. By George W. Cable.
Benjamin Franklin. By John Bach McMaster.
Edgar Allan Poe. By George E. Woodberry.
Each volume, with Portrait, 16mo, $1.25.
Others to be announced hereafter.

American Statesmen.

Edited by JOHN T. MORSE, Jr.
John Quincy Adams. By John T. Morse, Jr.
Alexander Hamilton. By Henry Cabot Lodge.
John C. Calhoun. By Dr. H. von Holst.
Andrew Jackson. By Prof. W. G. Sumner.
John Randolph. By Henry Adams.
James Monroe. By Pres. D. C. Gilman.
Thomas Jefferson. By John T. Morse, Jr.
Daniel Webster. By Henry Cabot Lodge.
Albert Gallatin. By John Austin Stevens.
(*In Preparation.*)
James Madison. By Sidney Howard Gay.
Patrick Henry. By Prof. Moses Coit Tyler.
Henry Clay. By Hon. Carl Schurz.
Each volume, 16mo, $1.25.
Others to be announced hereafter.

Mrs. Martha Babcock Amory.

Life of John Singleton Copley. 8vo, $3.00.

Hans Christian Andersen.

Complete Works. 10 vols. crown 8vo, each $1.50.

Francis, Lord Bacon.

Works. Collected and edited by Spedding, Ellis, and Heath.
15 vols. crown 8vo, $33.75.
Popular Edition. With Portraits and Index. 2 vols. crown
8vo, $5.00.
Promus of Formularies and Elegancies. 8vo, $5.00.
Life and Times of Bacon. Abridged. By James Spedding.
2 vols. crown 8vo, $5.00.

William Henry Bishop.

The House of a Merchant Prince. A Novel. 12mo, $1.50.
Detmold. A Novel. 18mo, $1.25.

Björnstjerne Björnson.

Norwegian Novels. 7 vols., 16mo, each $1.00.

British Poets.

Riverside Edition. Crown 8vo, each $1.75 ; the set, 68 vols.
$100.00.

Akenside and Beattie, 1 vol.
Ballads, 4 vols.
Burns, 1 vol.
Butler, 1 vol.
Byron, 5 vols.
Campbell and Falconer, 1 vol.
Chatterton, 1 vol.
Chaucer, 3 vols.
Churchill, Parnell, and Tickell, 2 vols.
Coleridge and Keats, 2 vols.
Cowper, 2 vols.
Dryden, 2 vols.
Gay, 1 vol.

Goldsmith and Gray, 1 vol.
Herbert and Vaughan, 1 vol.
Herrick, 1 vol.
Hood, 2 vols.
Milton and Marvell, 2 vols.
Montgomery, 2 vols.
Moore, 3 vols.
Pope and Collins, 2 vols.
Prior, 1 vol.
Scott, 5 vols.
Shakespeare and Jonson, 1 vol.
Shelley, 2 vols.
Skelton and Donne, 2 vols.
Southey, 5 vols.

Spenser, 3 vols.	Wordsworth, 3 vols.
Swift, 2 vols.	Wyatt and Surrey, 1 vol.
Thomson, 1 vol.	Young, 1 vol.
Watts and White, 1 vol.	

John Brown, M. D.

Spare Hours. 3 vols. 16mo, each $1.50.

Robert Browning.

Poems and Dramas, etc. 15 vols. 16mo, $20.50.
Complete Works. *New Edition.* 7 vols. crown 8vo, $12.00.
Jocoseria. New Poems. 16mo, $1.00. Crown 8vo, $1.00.

William Cullen Bryant.

Translation of Homer. The Iliad. 1 vol. crown 8vo, $3.00.
   2 vols. royal 8vo, $9.00 ; crown 8vo, $4.50.
The Odyssey. 1 vol. crown 8vo, $3.00. 2 vols. royal 8vo,
   $9.00 ; crown 8vo, $4.50.

Sara C. Bull.

Life of Ole Bull. Portrait and illustrations. 8vo, $2.50.

John Burroughs.

Wake-Robin. Illustrated.	Locusts and Wild Honey.
Winter Sunshine.	Pepacton, and Other Sketches.
Birds and Poets.	Each volume, 16mo, $1.50.

Thomas Carlyle.

Essays. With Portrait and Index. 4 vols. 12mo, $7.50.
   Popular Edition. 2 vols. 12mo, $3.50.

Alice and Phœbe Cary.

Poems. *Household Edition.* 12mo, $2.00.
Library Edition. Portraits and 24 illustrations. 8vo, $4.00.
Poetical Works, including Memorial by Mary Clemmer,
   8vo, full gilt, $4.00.

Lydia Maria Child.

Looking toward Sunset. 12mo, $2.50.
Letters. With Biography by Whittier. 16mo, $1.50.

James Freeman Clarke.
Ten Great Religions. 8vo, $3.00.
Ten Great Religions. Part II. Comparison of all Religions. 8vo, $3.00.
Common Sense in Religion. 12mo, $2.00.
Memorial and Biographical Sketches. 12mo, $2.00.

James Fenimore Cooper.
Works. *Household Edition.* Illustrated. 32 vols. 16mo, each $1.00; the set, $32.00.
Globe Edition. Illustrated. 16 vols. 16mo, $20.00. (*Sold only in sets.*)
Sea Tales. Illustrated. 10 vols. 16mo, $10.00.
Leather-Stocking Tales. *Household Edition.* Illustrated. 5 vols. 16mo, $5.00.

M. Creighton.
The Papacy during the Reformation. 2 vols. 8vo, $10.00.

Richard H. Dana.
To Cuba and Back. 16mo, $1.25.
Two Years before the Mast. 16mo, $1.50.

Thomas De Quincey.
Works. *Riverside Edition.* 12 vols. 12mo, each $1.50; the set, $18.00.
Globe Edition. 6 vols. 16mo, $10.00. (*Sold only in sets.*)

Madame De Staël.
Germany. 12mo, $2.50.

Charles Dickens.
Works. *Illustrated Library Edition.* With Dickens Dictionary. 30 vols. 12mo, each $1.50; the set, $45.00.
Globe Edition. 15 vols. 16mo, each $1.25.

J. Lewis Diman.
The Theistic Argument, etc. Crown 8vo, $2.00.
Orations and Essays. Crown 8vo, $2.50.

F. S. Drake.
Dictionary of American Biography. 8vo, $6.00.

Charles L. Eastlake.
Hints on Household Taste. Illustrated. 8vo, $3.00.
Notes on the Louvre and Brera Galleries. Small 4to, $2.00.

George Eliot.
The Spanish Gypsy. A Poem. 16mo, $1.50.

Ralph Waldo Emerson.
Works. *Riverside Edition.* 11 vols. each $1.75; the set, $19.25.
"*Little Classic*" *Edition.* 11 vols. 18mo, each, $1.50.
Parnassus. *Household Edition.* 12mo, $2.00.
Library Edition. 8vo, $4.00.

F. de S. de la Motte Fénelon.
Adventures of Telemachus. 12mo, $2.25.

James T. Fields.
Yesterdays with Authors. 12mo, $2.00. 8vo, $3.00.
Underbrush. 18mo, $1.25.
Ballads and other Verses. 16mo, $1.00.
The Family Library of British Poetry. Royal 8vo, $5.00.
Memoirs and Correspondence. 8vo, $2.00.

John Fiske.
Myths and Mythmakers. 12mo, $2.00.
Outlines of Cosmic Philosophy. 2 vols. 8vo, $6.00.
The Unseen World, and other Essays. 12mo, $2.00.
Excursions of an Evolutionist. (*In Press.*)

Dorsey Gardner.
Quatre Bras, Ligny and Waterloo. 8vo, $5.00.

Johann Wolfgang von Goethe.
Faust. Part First. Metrical Translation, by C. T. Brooks. 16mo, $1.25.
Faust. Translated by Bayard Taylor. 1 vol. crown 8vo, $3.00. 2 vols. royal 8vo, $9.00; crown 8vo, $4.50.
Correspondence with a Child. 12mo, $1.50.
Wilhelm Meister. Translated by Carlyle. 2 vols. 12mo, $3.00.

Arthur Sherburne Hardy.
But Yet a Woman. 16mo, $1.25.

Bret Harte.
Works. *New Edition.* 5 vols. Crown 8vo, each $2.00.
Poems. *Household Edition.* 12mo, $2.00. *Red Line Edition.* Small 4to, $2.50. *Diamond Edition,* $1.00.

Nathaniel Hawthorne.
Works. *"Little Classic"* Edition. Illustrated. 25 vols. 18mo, each $1.00 ; the set $25.00.
Fireside Edition. Illus. 13 vols. 16mo, the set, $21.00.
Globe Edition. Illustrated. 6 vols. 16mo, the set, $10.00.
New Riverside Edition. Introductions by G. P. Lathrop 11 Etchings and Portrait. 12 vols. crown 8vo, each $2.00

George S. Hillard.
Six Months in Italy. 12mo, $2.00.

Oliver Wendell Holmes.
Poems. *Household Edition.* 12mo, $2.00.
Illustrated Library Edition. 8vo, $4.00.
Handy-Volume Edition. 2 vols, 18mo, $2.50.
The Autocrat of the Breakfast-Table. Crown 8vo, $2.00.
Handy-Volume Edition. 18mo, $4.25.
The Professor at the Breakfast-Table. Crown 8vo, $2.00.
The Poet at the Breakfast-Table. Crown 8vo, $2.00.
Elsie Venner. Crown 8vo, $2.00.
The Guardian Angel. Crown 8vo, $2.00.
Medical Essays. Crown 8vo, $2.00.
Pages from an old Volume of Life. Crown 8vo, $2.00.
John Lothrop Motley. A Memoir. 16mo, $1.50.

Augustus Hoppin.
A Fashionable Sufferer. 12mo, $1.50.
Recollections of Auton House. 4to, $1.25.

William D. Howells.
Venetian Life. 12mo, $1.50.
Italian Journeys. 12mo, $1.50.
Their Wedding Journey. Illus. 12mo, $1.50 ; 18mo, $1.25.
Suburban Sketches. Illustrated. 12mo, $1.50.
A Chance Acquaintance. Illus. 12mo, $1.50 ; 18mo, $1.25.

A Foregone Conclusion. 12mo, $1.50.
The Lady of the Aroostook. 12mo, $1.50.
The Undiscovered Country. 12mo, $1.50.
Poems. 18mo, $1.25.
Out of the Question. A Comedy. 18mo, $1.25.
A Counterfeit Presentment. 18mo, $1.25.
Choice Autobiography. Edited by W. D. Howells.
8 vols. 18mo, each $1.25.

Thomas Hughes.

Tom Brown's School-Days at Rugby. 16mo, $1.00.
Tom Brown at Oxford. 16mo, $1.25.
The Manliness of Christ. 16mo, $1.00; paper, 25 cents.

William Morris Hunt.

Talks on Art. Series I. and II. 8vo, each $1.00.

Henry James, Jr.

A Passionate Pilgrim and other Tales. 12mo, $2.00.
Transatlantic Sketches. 12mo, $2.00.
Roderick Hudson. 12mo, $2.00.
The American. 12mo, $2.00.
Watch and Ward. 18mo, $1.25.
The Europeans. 12mo, $1.50.
Confidence. 12mo, $1.50.
The Portrait of a Lady. 12mo, $2.00.

Mrs. Anna Jameson.

Writings upon Art Subjects. 10 vols. 18mo, each $1.50.

Sarah Orne Jewett.

Deephaven. 18mo, $1.25.
Old Friends and New. 18mo, $1.25.
Country By-Ways. 18mo, $1.25.
Play-Days. Stories for Children. Square 16mo, $1.50.
The Mate of the Daylight. (*In Press.*)

Rossiter Johnson.

Little Classics. Eighteen handy volumes containing the
choicest Stories, Sketches, and short Poems in English
Literature. Each in one vol. 18mo, $1.00 ; the set, $18.00.
9 vols., square 16mo, $13.50. (*Sold only in sets.*)

Samuel Johnson.
Oriental Religions : India, 8vo, $5.00. China, 8vo, $5.00.
Persia, 8vo. (*In Press.*)
Lectures, Essays, and Sermons. Crown 8vo, $1.75.

T. Starr King.
Christianity and Humanity. With Portrait. 16mo, $2.00.
Substance and Show. 16mo, $2.00.

Lucy Larcom.
Poems. 16mo, $1.25.
An Idyl of Work. 16mo, $1.25.
Wild Roses of Cape Ann and other Poems. 16mo, $1.25.
Breathings of the Better Life. 16mo, $1.25.

George Parsons Lathrop.
A Study of Hawthorne. 18mo, $1.25.
An Echo of Passion. 16mo, $1.25.

Charles G. Leland.
The Gypsies. Crown 8vo, $2.00.

George Henry Lewes.
The Story of Goethe's Life. Portrait. 12mo, $1.50.
Problems of Life and Mind. 5 vols. 8vo, $14.00.

Henry Wadsworth Longfellow.
Poems. *Cambridge Edition.* Portrait. 4 vols. 12mo, $9.00.
 2 vols. 12mo, $7.00.
Octavo Edition. Portrait and 300 illustrations. $8.00.
Household Edition. Portrait. 12mo, $2.00.
Red-Line Edition. Portrait and 12 illus. Small 4to, $2.50.
Diamond Edition. $1.00.
Library Edition. Portrait and 32 illustrations. 8vo, $4.00.
Christus. *Household Edition,* $2.00 ; *Diamond Edition,* $1.00.
Prose Works. *Cambridge Edition.* 2 vols. 12mo, $4.50.
Hyperion. A Romance. 16mo, $1.50 ; paper, 15 cents.
Kavanagh. 16mo, $1.50.
Outre-Mer. 16mo, $1.50, paper, 15 cents.
In the Harbor. Portrait. 16mo, $1.00.

Michael Angelo ; a Drama. Illustrated. Folio. (*In Press.*)
Twenty Poems. Illustrated. Small 4to, $4.00.
Translation of the Divina Commedia of Dante. 1 vol.
    cr. 8vo, $3.00. 3 vols. royal 8vo, $13.50 ; cr. 8vo, $6.00.
Poets and Poetry of Europe. Royal 8vo, $5.00.

James Russell Lowell.
Poems. *Red-Line Edition.* Portrait. Illus. Small 4to, $2.50.
Household Edition. Portrait. 12mo, $2.00.
Library Edition. Portrait and 32 illustrations. 8vo, $4.00.
Diamond Edition. $1.00.
Fireside Travels. 12mo, $1.50.
Among my Books. Series I. and II. 12mo, each $2.00.
My Study Windows. 12mo, $2.00.

Thomas Babington Macaulay.
England. *Riverside Edition.* 4 vols. 12mo, $5.00.
Essays. Portrait. *Riverside Edition.* 3 vols. 12mo, $3.75.
Speeches and Poems. *Riverside Edition.* 12mo, $1.25.

Harriet Martineau.
Autobiography. Portraits and illus. 2 vols. 8vo, $6.00.
Household Education. 18mo, $1.25.

Owen Meredith.
Poems. *Household Edition.* Illustrated. 12mo, $2.00.
Library Edition. Portrait and 32 illustrations. 8vo, $4.00.
Shawmut Edition. 16mo, $1.50.
Lucile. *Red-Line Edition.* 8 illustrations. Small 4to, $2.50.
Diamond Edition. 8 illustrations. $1.00.

J. W. Mollett.
Illustrated Dictionary of Words used in Art and Archæ-
    ology. Small 4to, $5.00.

Michael de Montaigne.
Complete Works. Portrait. 4 vols. 12mo, $7.50.

William Mountford.
Euthanasy. 12mo, $2.00.

T. Mozley.
Reminiscences of Oriel College, etc. 2 vols. 16mo, $3.00.

Elisha Mulford.
The Nation. 8vo, $2.50.
The Republic of God. 8vo, $2.00.

T. T. Munger.
On the Threshold. 16mo, $1.00.
The Freedom of Faith. 16mo, $1.50.

J A. W. Neander.
History of the Christian Religion and Church, with Index volume, 6 vols. 8vo, $20.00 ; Index alone, $3.00.

Charles Eliot Norton.
Notes of Travel and Study in Italy. 16mo, $1.25.
Translation of Dante's New Life. Royal 8vo, $3.00.

Francis W. Palfrey.
Memoir of William Francis Bartlett. 16mo, $1.50.

James Parton.
Life of Benjamin Franklin. 2 vols. 8vo, $4.00.
Life of Thomas Jefferson. 8vo, $2.00.
Life of Aaron Burr. 2 vols. $4.00.
Life of Andrew Jackson. 3 vols. 8vo, $6.00.
Life of Horace Greeley. 8vo, $2.50.
General Butler in New Orleans. 8vo, $2.50.
Humorous Poetry of the English Language. 8vo, $2.00.
Famous Americans of Recent Times. 8vo, $2.00.
Life of Voltaire. 2 vols. 8vo, $6.00.
The French Parnassus. 12mo, $2.00 ; crown 8vo, $3.50.

Blaise Pascal.
Thoughts, Letters, and Opuscules. 12mo, $2.25.
Provincial Letters. 12mo, $2.25.

Elizabeth Stuart Phelps.
The Gates Ajar. 16mo, $1.50.
Beyond the Gates. 16mo, $1.25.
Men, Women, and Ghosts. 16mo, $1.50.
Hedged In. 16mo, $1.50.

The Silent Partner. 16mo, $1.50.
The Story of Avis. 16mo, $1.50.
Sealed Orders, and other Stories. 16mo, $1.50.
Friends; A Duet. 16mo, $1.25.
Doctor Zay. 16mo, $1.25.
Poetic Studies. Square 16mo, $1.50.

Carl Ploetz.

Epitome of Ancient, Mediæval and Modern History. (*In Press.*)

Adelaide A. Procter.

Poems. *Diamond Edition.* $1.00.
Red-Line Edition. Portrait and illus. Small 4to, $2.50.

Henry Crabb Robinson.

Diary, Reminiscences, etc. Crown 8vo, $2.50.

A. P. Russell.

Library Notes. Crown 8vo, $2.00.
Characteristics. Crown 8vo. (*In Press.*)

John Godfrey Saxe.

Works. Portrait. 16mo, $2.25.
Poems. *Red-Line Edition.* Illustrated. Small 4to, $2.50.
Diamond Edition. $1.00.
Household Edition. 12mo, $2.00.

Sir Walter Scott.

Waverley Novels. *Illustrated Library Edition.* 25 vols. 12mo, each $1.00 ; the set, $25.00.
Globe Edition. 100 illustrations. 13 vols. 16mo, $16.25.
Tales of a Grandfather. *Library Edition.* 3 vols. 12mo, $4.50.
Poems. *Red-Line Edition.* Illustrated. Small 4to, $2.50.
Diamond Edition. $1.00.

Horace E. Scudder.

The Bodley Books. Illus. 7 vols. Small 4to, each $1.50.
The Dwellers in Five-Sisters' Court. 16mo, $1.25.
Stories and Romances. 16mo, $1.25.
Dream Children. Illustrated. 16mo, $1.00.

Seven Little People. Illustrated. 16mo, $1.00.
Stories from my Attic. Illustrated. 16mo, $1.00.
The Children's Book. Illustrated. 4to, 450 pages, $3.50.
Boston Town. Illustrated. 12mo, $1.50.

W. H. Seward.
Works. 5 vols. (*In Press.*)
Diplomatic History of the War. 8vo, $3.00.

John Campbell Shairp.
Culture and Religion. 16mo, $1.25.
Poetic Interpretation of Nature. 16mo, $1.25.
Studies in Poetry and Philosophy. 16mo, $1.50.
Aspects of Poetry. 16mo, $1.50.

William Shakespeare.
Works ; edited by R. G. White. *Riverside Edition.* 3 vols. crown 8vo, each, $2.50.
The Same. 6 vols. 8vo, each $2.50. (*In Press.*)

Dr. William Smith.
Bible Dictionary. *American Edition.* The set, 4 vols. 8vo, $20.00.

James Spedding.
Evenings with a Reviewer. 2 vols. 8vo, $7.00.

Edmund Clarence Stedman.
Poems. *Farringford Edition.* Portrait. 16mo, $2.00.
Victorian Poets. 12mo, $2.00.
Hawthorne, and other Poems. 16mo, $1.25.
Edgar Allan Poe. An Essay. Vellum, 18mo, $1.00.
Elizabeth Barrett Browning. An Essay. 18mo, 75cts.

Harriet Beecher Stowe.
Agnes of Sorrento. 12mo, $1.50.
The Pearl of Orr's Island. 12mo, $1.50.
The Minister's Wooing. 12mo, $1.50.
The May-flower, and other Sketches. 12mo, $1.50.
Nina Gordon. 12mo, $1.50.
Oldtown Folks. 12mo, $1.50.
Sam Lawson's Fireside Stories. Illustrated. 12mo, $1.50.

Uncle Tom's Cabin. 100 Illustrations. 12mo, $3.50.
Popular Edition. 12mo, $2.00.

Bayard Taylor.
Poetical Works. *Household Edition.* 12mo, $2.00.
Dramatic Works. 12mo, $2.25.
The Echo Club. 18mo, $1.25.

Alfred Tennyson.
Poems. *Household Edition.* Portrait and illus. 12mo, $2.00.
Illustrated Crown Edition. 2 vols. 8vo, $5.00.
Library Edition. Portrait and 60 illustrations. 8vo, $4.00.
Red-Line Edition. Portrait and illus. Small 4to, $2.50.
Diamond Edition. $1.00.
Shawmut Edition. Illustrated. 16mo, $1.50.
Idylls of the King. Illustrated. 12mo, $1.50.

Celia Thaxter.
Among the Isles of Shoals. 18mo, $1.25.
Poems. Small 4to, $1.50.
Drift-Weed. Poems. 18mo, $1.50.
Poems for Children. Illustrated. (*In Press.*)

Henry D. Thoreau.
Works. 8 vols. 12mo, each $1.50 ; the set, $12.00.

George Ticknor.
History of Spanish Literature. 3 vols. 8vo, $10.00.
Life, Letters, and Journals. Portraits. 2 vols. 8vo, $6.00.
Cheaper Edition. 2 vols. 12mo, $4.00.

J. T. Trowbridge.
A Home Idyl. 16mo, $1.25.
The Vagabonds. 16mo, $1.25.
The Emigrant's Story. 16mo, $1.25.

Herbert Tuttle.
History of Prussia. (*In Press.*)

Jones Very.
Poems. With Memoir. 16mo, $1.50.

F. M. A. de Voltaire.
History of Charles XII. 12mo, $2.25.

Lew Wallace.
The Fair God. A Novel. 12mo, $1.50.

Charles Dudley Warner.
My Summer in a Garden. 16mo, $1.00.
Illustrated Edition. Square 16mo, $1.50.
Saunterings. 18mo, $1.25.
Back-Log Studies. Illustrated. Square 16mo, $1.50.
Baddeck, and that sort of Thing. 18mo, $1.00.
My Winter on the Nile. Crown 8vo, $2.00.
In the Levant. Crown 8vo, $2.00.
Being a Boy. Illustrated. Square 16mo, $1.50.
In the Wilderness. 18mo, 75 cents.
A Roundabout Journey. (*In Press.*)

William A. Wheeler.
Dictionary of Noted Names of Fiction. 12mo, $2.00.

Edwin P. Whipple.
Literature and Life.
Essays and Reviews. 2 vols.
Character and Characteristic Men.
The Literature of the Age of Elizabeth.
Success and its Conditions.
6 vols. crown 8vo, each $1.50.

Richard Grant White.
Every-Day English. 12mo, $2.00.
Words and their Uses. 12mo, $2.00.
England Without and Within. 12mo, $2.00.

Mrs. A D. T. Whitney.
Faith Gartney's Girlhood. 12mo, $1.50.
Hitherto. 12mo, $1.50.
Patience Strong's Outings. 12mo, $1.50.
The Gayworthys. 12mo, $1.50.
Leslie Goldthwaite. Illustrated. 12mo, $1.50.
We Girls. Illustrated. 12mo, $1.50.

Real Folks. Illustrated. 12mo, $1.50.
The Other Girls. Illustrated. 12mo, $1.50.
Sights and Insights. 2 vols. 12mo, $3.00.
Odd or Even. 12mo, $1.50.
Boys at Chequasset. 12mo, $1.50.
Mother Goose for Grown Folks. 12mo, $1.50.
Zerub Throop's Experiment. 12mo, $1.50. (*In Press.*)
Pansies. Square 16mo, $1.50.
Just How. 16mo, $1.00.

John Greenleaf Whittier.

Poems. *Household Edition.* Portrait. 12mo, $2.00.
Cambridge Edition. Portrait. 3 vols. 12mo, $6.75.
Red-Line Edition. Portrait. Illustrated. Small 4to, $2.50.
Diamond Edition. $1.00.
Library Edition. Portrait. 32 illustrations. 8vo, $4.00.
Prose Works. *Cambridge Edition.* 2 vols. 12mo, $4.50.
John Woolman's Journal. Introduction by Whittier. $1.50.
Child Life in Poetry. Selected by Whittier. Illustrated.
    16mo, $2.25. Child Life in Prose. 16mo, $2.25.
Songs of Three Centuries. Selected by J. G. Whittier.
    Household Edition. 12mo, $2.00.
    Illustrated Library Edition. 32 illustrations. 8vo, $4.00.

J. A. Wilstach.

Translation of Virgil's Works. 2 vols. cr. 8vo. (*In Press.*)

Justin Winsor.

Reader's Handbook of American Revolution. 16mo, $1.25.

J. H. D. Zschokke.

Meditations on Life, Death, and Eternity. Cr. 8vo, $2.00.

A catalogue containing portraits of many of the above authors, with a description of their works, will be sent free, on application, to any address.

HOUGHTON, MIFFLIN AND COMPANY,

4 PARK ST., BOSTON.   11 EAST 17TH ST., NEW YORK.